A New True Book

AFRICA

By D.V. Georges

CHILDRENS PRESS ®

CHICAGO

This biracial group of students represents the
five major ethnic groups that live in Africa today.

PHOTO CREDITS

© Cameramann International, Ltd.—2,
20 (right), 42, 44 (left)

Gartman Agency: © Wally Hampton—
9 (right)

© Virginia Grimes—30 (right)

Historical Pictures Service,
Chicago—36

Nawrocki Stock Photo:
© Jason Lauré—9 (left), 12 (right)
© Leslie C. Street—10 (right)
© D. J. Variakojis—10 (left)

Odyssey Productions, Chicago:
© Robert Frerck—13 (2 photos), 14
(right), 22 (right), 25 (left), 30 (left), 33
(right), 41 (right)

Photri—17, 19, 22 (left), 25 (right), 44
(right)

R/C Agency:
© Richard L. Capps—33 (left)
© Betty Kubis—28 (top left)

© H. Armstrong Roberts—Cover

Roloc Color Slides—26

© James P. Rowan—34 (right)

Tom Stack & Associates:
© C. Benjamin—16 (top)
© Fawcett—28 (bottom right), 37
(right)
© Warren & Genny Garst—27 (right)
© F.S. Mitchell—28 (top right), 41 (left)
© Brian Parker—27 (left)
© Leonard Lee Rue III—28 (bottom
left)

Valan Photos:
© Kennon Cooke—39 (left)
© Stephen J. Krasemann—29, 37
(left)
© Val and Alan Wilkinson—8

Library of Congress Cataloging-in-Publication Data

Georges, D. V.
    Africa.

    (A New true book)
    Includes index.
    Summary: Briefly describes Africa's regions: North
Africa, the Sahara, the equatorial rain forest, the west
coast, east Africa, island countries off the southeast
coast, and southern Africa.
    1. Africa—Juvenile literature. [1. Africa—
Geography] I. Title.
DT6.G46 1986   916   86-9586
ISBN 0-516-01287-8

TABLE OF CONTENTS

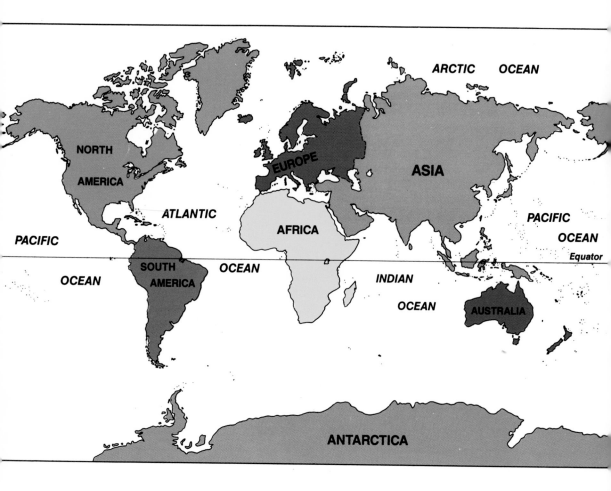

ARCTIC   OCEAN

NORTH
AMERICA

EUROPE

ASIA

ATLANTIC

AFRICA

PACIFIC
OCEAN

PACIFIC

OCEAN

SOUTH
AMERICA

OCEAN

INDIAN

Equator

OCEAN

OCEAN

AUSTRALIA

ANTARCTICA

FINDING AFRICA

A continent is a huge mass of land.

There are seven continents. Of the seven, Africa is the second largest. Only Asia is a larger continent. (The other five continents are North America, South America, Europe, Australia, and Antarctica.)

Africa is near Asia and Europe. The Gulf of Aden, the Red Sea, and the Suez Canal separate Africa from Asia. The Mediterranean Sea and the Strait of Gibraltar separate Africa from Europe.

Oceans surround the rest of Africa. To the west, the Atlantic Ocean stretches along 6,500 miles of coastline. On Africa's east coast, the Indian Ocean coastline is 4,000 miles long.

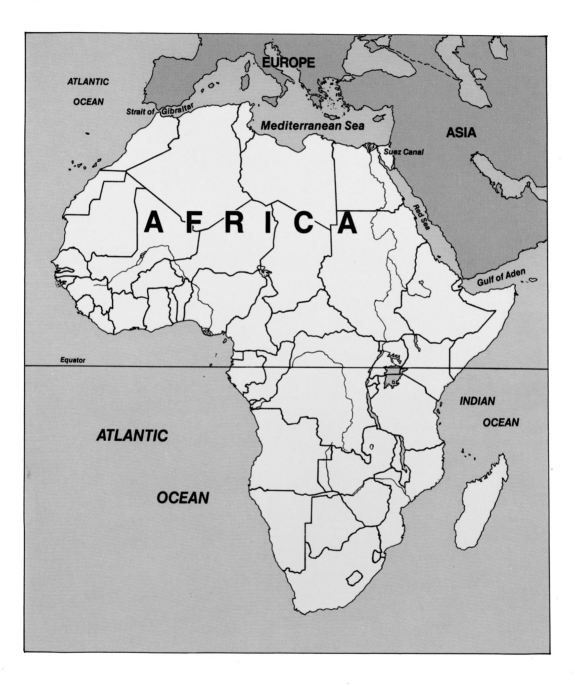

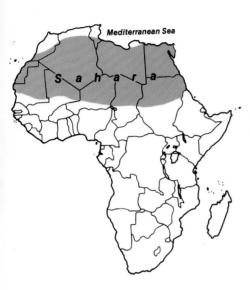

Mediterranean Sea

S a h a r a

Sand dunes in the Sahara can be hundreds of feet high.

A great desert covers more than one fourth of Africa. It is the Sahara, the largest desert in the world. The Sahara begins near Africa's Mediterranean coast and covers 1,200 miles of land to the south.

Children of Ismailia, Egypt (left) and a girl
from the Pokot tribe that lives in north-central Kenya.

In the desert countries
live Egyptians, Berbers,
and Arabs. However, most
Africans live south of
the Sahara.

Early explorers knew of
northern Africa and its
people. However, the great
Sahara prevented travel
south. Africa's interior was

9

Game park (above) and
Lake Nakuru (right) in Kenya

a mystery. Because of this,
it was called "the dark
continent."

Eventually, explorers
discovered that Africa was
a land of great beauty and
natural riches.

NORTH AFRICA

The five countries of Morocco, Algeria, Tunisia, Libya, and Egypt are in North Africa. These countries lie along the coast of the Mediterranean Sea.

Over one thousand years ago, Arabs entered North Africa from Arabia, in Asia.

A man calls the Muslims to prayer.
Muslims pray five times a day.

Long before the Arabs
came, Berbers and
Egyptians lived in North
Africa. Today, Berbers,
Egyptians, and Arabs have
the same religion, called
Islam. People who believe
in Islam are Muslims.

Most of North Africa is a hot desert. However, in the Atlas Mountains, near the northwestern coast, summers are hot, but winters are cool and rainy. Farmers grow fruit, vegetables, and wheat.

Village (below) and farm fields (left) in the Atlas Mountains

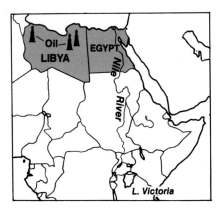

Traditional Egyptian sailboats, called
feluccas, still sail on the Nile River

To the east, almost all of
Libya and Egypt is desert.
However, Libya is rich in
oil. Money from oil helps
to improve farming. In
Egypt, water from the Nile
River is used for irrigation.

The Nile is the longest
river in the world. It begins

at Lake Victoria, four thousand miles from its mouth.

Around 5000 B.C., the ancient Egyptians began irrigation near the Nile. They built canals to take water from the river to fields. Thus, more food could grow.

Ancient Egyptians were great engineers and architects. Along the banks of the Nile they built pyramids from large blocks

The pyramids in Giza (right) attract thousands of tourists every year.

of stone. Together, the blocks weighed many tons. One pyramid could take twenty years to build! The most famous pyramids are in Giza, near Cairo.

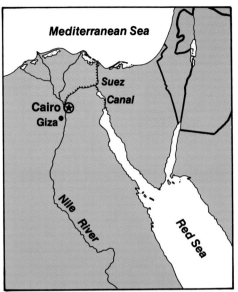

Ships wait to go
through the Suez Canal.

In 1869, the Suez Canal
was built. It connects the
Red Sea with the
Mediterranean Sea. Before,
ships from the West had
to sail around Africa to
reach the Far East. The
Suez Canal shortened this
trip by ten thousand miles.

17

THE SAHARA

Because rainfall is low, very little grows or lives in the Sahara. Most of the Sahara is barren mountains and rocky plains.

In parts of the Sahara, sand dunes cover the land. Strong desert winds carried the sand from mountains and plains to these places. Some sand dunes are seven hundred feet high!

The plains and sand dunes are usually hot. But

high in the mountains,
temperatures can reach
freezing.

In some places,
underground water flows
up to the earth's surface.
Where this happens, plants
grow, and an oasis forms.

Djanet Oasis in the Sahara

Nomads travel across the desert sands as their ancestors did hundreds of years before.

Many nomads live in the Sahara. They raise herds of sheep, goats, and cattle. After the herds eat all the grass in one part of the desert, nomads move to a new grassy place. Nomads move often.

Not all people in the Sahara are nomads. Some people live permanently near an oasis, where they grow dates and vegetables.

Desert people travel to Timbuktu, in the south Sahara, to buy supplies. Hundreds of years ago, Timbuktu was a great city. People from north and south met there to buy and sell gold. The gold came from Burkina Faso and Ghana, to the south.

Arabian camel with its young (above)
and a camel market (right)

Most desert people use
Arabian camels for travel.
The Arabian camel, which
has one hump, is also
called a dromedary. In its
hump, the dromedary
stores fat. It does not store
water. However, it can go

for days without drinking.
Then, it can drink twenty
gallons of water at once!

South of the Sahara is a
region called the Sahel.
Rainfall there is higher
than on the desert, so
more plants and trees
grow. Sometimes, though,
rain may not fall for five
years or more. Then, there
is often not enough food.

THE RAIN FOREST OF EQUATORIAL AFRICA

The equator runs through the very middle of Africa. This region is called equatorial Africa.

Because rain falls almost every day, trees grow tall. Tropical vines, called

Rain forest near Victoria Falls (left).
A volcano (right) looms beyond this rain forest in Zaire.

lianas, crawl up through
the trees. Much of
equatorial Africa is a hot
rain forest.

25

Group of pygmies photographed on the road to the Itum Forest.

The great Zaire, Africa's second-longest river, flows through the rain forest. Along the Zaire live pygmies, who are less than five feet tall.

Pygmies are skilled

Lowland Gorilla   Chimpanzee

hunters. They also gather
food from forest plants.

In the rain forest live the
gorilla, the largest of apes,
and the chimpanzee, the
smartest of apes.

The hippopotamus
spends much time in
rivers, with only its eyes
and nose above water.

Lion

Hippopotamus

Gemsbok or oryx

Gerenuk

Wildlife is Africa's greatest national treasure.
Unfortunately as people take the land for increased
agricultural and industrial production many
animals lose their feeding grounds. Some,
such as the gorilla, have become endangered species.

North and south of the rain forest, less rain falls. Instead of trees, different kinds of grass grow. The grassy places are called savannas. Some savanna grass grows twelve feet high!

Giraffes roam the grasslands.

Oil rig off Port Harcourt, Nigeria (above)
and ripe cacao pods (right)

Many products come from equatorial Africa. Palm nuts and cacao beans grow there. Palm nuts contain palm oil, which is used in making soap. From the cacao bean comes cocoa. Along the Atlantic coast, oil has been discovered.

COAST OF IVORY, GOLD, AND SLAVES

In 1434, explorers from Portugal began sailing down Africa's west coast.

Prince Henry the Navigator sent the first explorers. He had heard of gold, ivory, and other riches from Africa. Also, he wanted to find a new route to the Far East. Eventually, explorers from Great Britain and Holland followed the Portuguese.

Explorers called part of the coast the "ivory coast," because of the ivory carvings the Africans made there. Today, this coast is part of the Republic of the Ivory Coast.

Ghana's coast was called the "gold coast." Africans traded gold for goods from Europe.

The "slave coast" was close by. Africans were taken as slaves to other parts of the world. Benin, Togo, and Nigeria are

Ceremonial ax (right) in the National Museum in Accra,
Ghana and the African mask (left) are examples of African art.

countries whose coasts
once were part of the
slave coast.

Today, Nigeria is a great
oil producer. Ghana exports
much gold. The Republic
of the Ivory Coast exports
mahogany and teak, fine
woods used for furniture.

Mount Kilimanjaro, Kenya

EAST AFRICA

The highest mountains are in East Africa. Mount Kilimanjaro rises to almost twenty thousand feet. It is always snowcapped.

There are many lakes in the mountains of East

Africa. Lake Victoria is the largest. In fact, Lake Victoria is the second-largest freshwater lake in the world.

Lake Nyasa, Lake Tanganyika, and Lake Rudolf are other large lakes in the mountains. They are long and deep. In places, Lake Tanganyika is 4,700 feet deep!

In the 1860s, the British missionary Dr. David Livingstone explored the lakes of East Africa. He

Dr. David Livingstone was the first European to explore the interior of East Africa.

wanted to learn about Africa's interior. From reports of his travels, he hoped people would understand Africa better. Also, he wanted his reports to help end the slave trade. The Livingstone Mountains in Tanzania are named for him.

Grant's zebras and elephants
are some of the animals protected
from hunters.

Every year, many people
visit Tanzania and Kenya.
Both countries have
pleasant weather and large
animal reserves.

Giraffes, elephants,
gazelles, and zebras are
some of the animals
protected from hunters.

ISLAND COUNTRIES OF SOUTHEAST AFRICA

Madagascar lies off the southeast coast of Africa. It is the world's fourth-largest island. Madagascar exports more vanilla than any other country.

Between Madagascar and Africa's coast are the Comoros. These small

Ring-tailed lemur

islands are a separate country.

Lemurs, which are relatives of monkeys, live only on Madagascar and the Comoros. Lemurs have large eyes and long, furry tails. Most lemurs live in trees. But the ring-tailed lemur lives on the ground.

SOUTHERN AFRICA

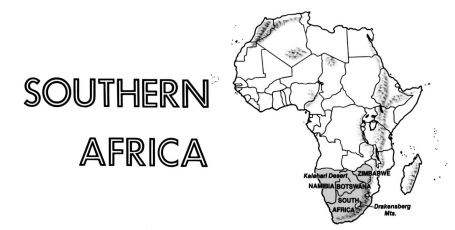

Botswana, Zimbabwe, Namibia, and South Africa are important mining countries in southern Africa. These countries export diamonds, gold, and silver to much of the rest of the world.

Most of southern Africa is hot. The Kalahari Desert is in Botswana.

Kalahari bush people (left) in
Botswana. Bantu miners (above) drilling
in a gold mine in South Africa

The San live in the
Kalahari Desert. Non-
Africans call these people
Bushmen. The San are
hunters. They also gather
food from desert plants.

In Zimbabwe, many
people visit Victoria Falls
National Park. Dr. David
Livingstone discovered

Victoria Falls on the Zambezi River in Zimbabwe are one mile wide.

Victoria Falls, on the
Zambezi River, in 1855.

Near the coast of South
Africa lie the Drakensberg
Mountains. The climate is
cool and rainy. Land along
this coast is good for
farming and cattle raising.

AFRICA'S FUTURE

Before 1960, only a few countries in Africa were independent. Most of Africa was governed by Portugal, France, Belgium, and Great Britain.

Africans fought many wars to become free. Since 1960, over forty independent countries have been formed in Africa.

Bridge crossing the Nile River into downtown Cairo, the capital of Egypt, and a native village in Kenya (right) clearly demonstrate the old and new face of Africa.

Today, many of these countries are poor.

But Africa has many natural riches. With time, the new countries will grow and develop.

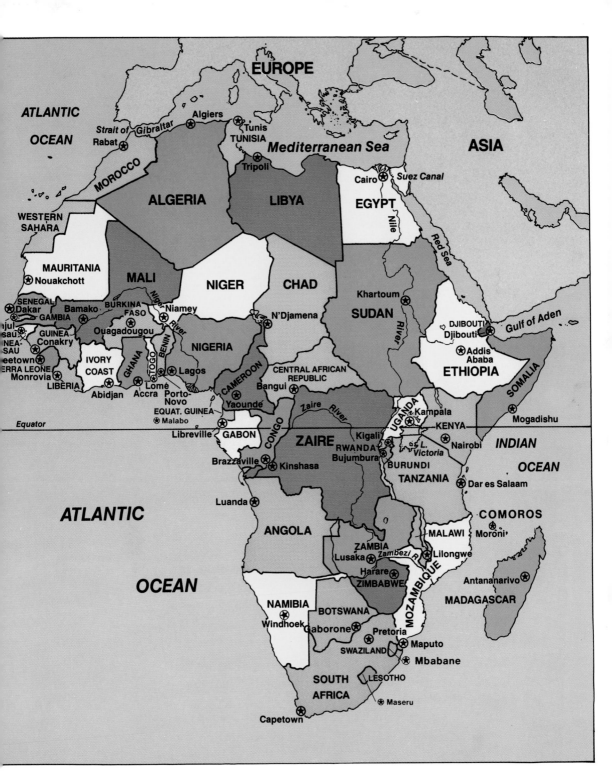

WORDS YOU SHOULD KNOW

ancient(AIN • chent)—of a very long time ago

canal(kah • NAL)—a narrow channel, dug out of land, that connects two seas or that takes river water to fields or farms

desert(DEZ • ert)—a place where little rain falls and few plants grow

equator(ih • KWAY • ter)—an imaginary geographical line that divides the Northern Hemisphere from the Southern Hemisphere

equatorial Africa(ek • wah • TOR • ee • il AFF • rih • kah)—the part of Africa that is near the equator

export(X • port)—to send something to another country for sale there

interior(in • TEER • ee • or)—land inside a country's coasts or borders

irrigation(ear • ih • GAY • shun)—moving water from a river to a field

missionary(MISH • un • air • ee)—a person who travels to distant lands to teach religion to the people there

oasis(oh • AY • siss)—a place in the desert where there are water and plants

pyramids(PEER • rah • midz)—large stone buildings that have a square base and four triangle-shaped sides

rain forest(RAYN FOR • ist)—a tall forest that grows in a very rainy climate

reserve(re • ZERV)—a large park for animals, where people cannot hunt

sand dune(SAND DOON)—a hill of sand caused by the wind

savanna(suh • VAN • ah)—an area in a warm climate where much grass grows

MAJOR COUNTRIES IN AFRICA

Name	Date of Independence	Capital
Algeria	(1962)	Algiers
Angola	(1975)	Luanda
Benin	(1960)	Porto-Novo
Botswana	(1966)	Gaborone
Burkina Faso	(1960)	Ouagadougou
Burundi	(1962)	Bujumbura
Cameroon	(1960)	Yaoundé
Canary Islands (Spanish)		Santa Cruz de Tenerife; Las Palmas
Cape Verde	(1975)	Praia
Central African Republic	(1960)	Bangui
Chad	(1960)	N'Djamena
Comoros	(1975)	Moroni
Congo	(1960)	Brazzaville
Djibouti	(1977)	Djibouti
Egypt	(1922)	Cairo
Equatorial Guinea	(1968)	Malabo
Ethiopia		Addis Ababa
Gabon	(1960)	Libreville
Gambia	(1965)	Banjul
Ghana	(1957)	Accra
Guinea	(1958)	Conakry
Guinea-Bissau	(1974)	Bissau
Ivory Coast	(1960)	Abidjan
Kenya	(1963)	Nairobi
Lesotho	(1966)	Maseru
Liberia	(1847)	Monrovia
Libya	(1951)	Tripoli
Madagascar	(1960)	Antananarivo
Malawi	(1964)	Lilongwe
Mali	(1960)	Bamako
Mauritania	(1960)	Nouakchott
Mauritius	(1968)	Port Louis de Gran Canaria
Madeira Islands (Portugese)		Funchal
Morocco	(1956)	Rabat
Mozambique	(1975)	Maputo
Namibia (South West Africa) (controlled by South Africa)		Windhoek
Niger	(1960)	Niamey
Nigeria	(1960)	Lagos
Reunion (French)		Saint-Denis
Rwanda	(1962)	Kigali
São Tomé and Principe	(1975)	São Tomé
Senegal	(1960)	Dakar
Seychelles	(1976)	Victoria
Sierra Leone	(1961)	Freetown
Somalia	(1960)	Mogadishu
South Africa	(1931)	Cape Town; Pretoria; Bloemfontein
Sudan	(1956)	Khartoum
Swaziland	(1968)	Mbabane
Tanzania	(1964)	Dar es Salaam
Togo	(1960)	Lomé
Tunisia	(1956)	Tunis
Uganda	(1962)	Kampala
Western Sahara (disputed)		None
Zaire	(1960)	Kinshasa
Zambia	(1964)	Lusaka
Zimbabwe	(1980)	Harare

INDEX

About the author

D.V. Georges is a geophysicist in Houston, Texas. Dr. Georges attended Rice University, earning a masters degree in chemistry in 1975 and a doctorate in geophysics in 1978.